© 2008 by Faber Music Ltd
First published by Faber Music Ltd in 2008
3 Queen Square, London WC1N 3AU

Arranged by Neil Williams
Engraved by Tom Fleming
Edited by Lucy Holliday & Alex Davis

Guitar by Tom Fleming
Bass by Neil Williams
Drums by Noam Lederman
Mixed & Engineered by Phil Hilborne

Noam is endorsed by
Mapex, Paiste & Protection Racket

Designed by Lydia Merrills-Ashcroft
Photographs © Referns Music Library

Printed in England by Caligraving Ltd
All rights reserved

The text paper used in this publication is a virgin fibre product that is manufactured in the UK to ISO 14001 standards. The wood fibre used is only sourced from managed forests using sustainable forestry principles. This paper is 100% recyclable

ISBN10: 0-571-53164-4
EAN13: 978-0-571-53164-6

Reproducing this music in any form is illegal & forbidden by the Copyright, Designs and Patents Act, 1988

To buy Faber Music publications or to find out about the full range of titles available, please contact your local music retailer or Faber Music sales enquiries:

Faber Music Ltd, Burnt Mill, Elizabeth Way,
Harlow, CM20 2HX England
Tel:+44(0)1279 82 89 82
Fax:+44(0)1279 82 89 83
sales@fabermusic.com fabermusic.com

TUNING NOTES CD 01

I CAN SEE FOR MILES
PAGE 04: CD 02/03

I CAN'T EXPLAIN
PAGE 10: CD 04/05

THE KIDS ARE ALRIGHT
PAGE 15: CD 06/07

MY GENERATION
PAGE 20: CD 08/09

PINBALL WIZARD
PAGE 28: CD 10/11

SUBSTITUTE
PAGE 34: CD 12/13

PICTURES OF LILY
PAGE 40: CD 14/15

WON'T GET FOOLED AGAIN
PAGE 45: CD 16/17

ON THE CD: FIRST VERSION OF SONG IS THE FULL DEMONSTRATION TRACK, THE SECOND VERSION IS THE BACKING TRACK TO PLAY ALONG TO

I CAN SEE FOR MILES

Words and Music by Pete Townshend

© 1967 Fabulous Music Ltd

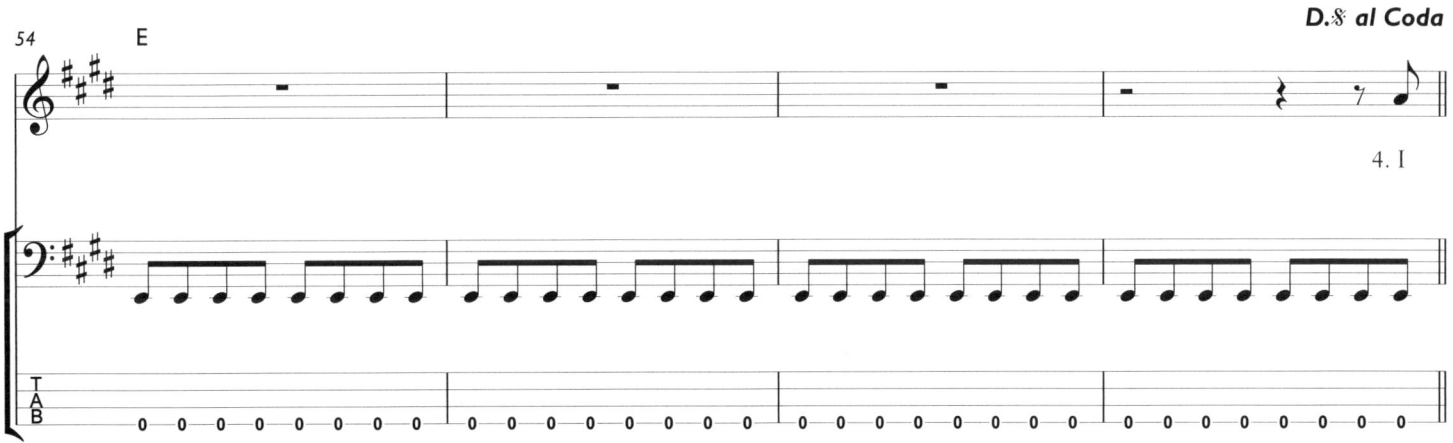
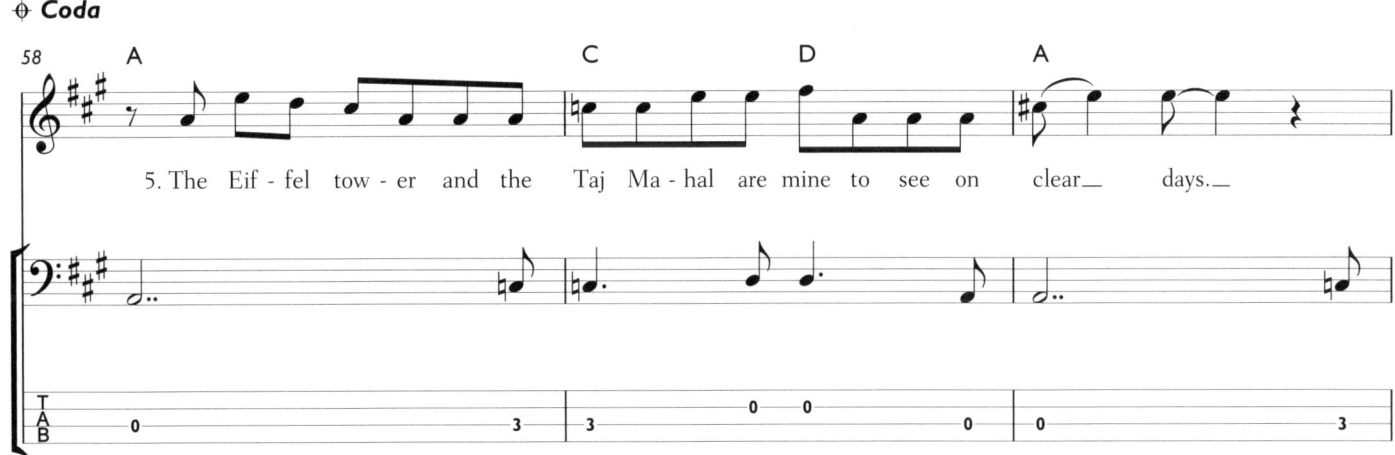

I CAN'T EXPLAIN

Words and Music by Pete Townshend

© 1965 Fabulous Music Ltd

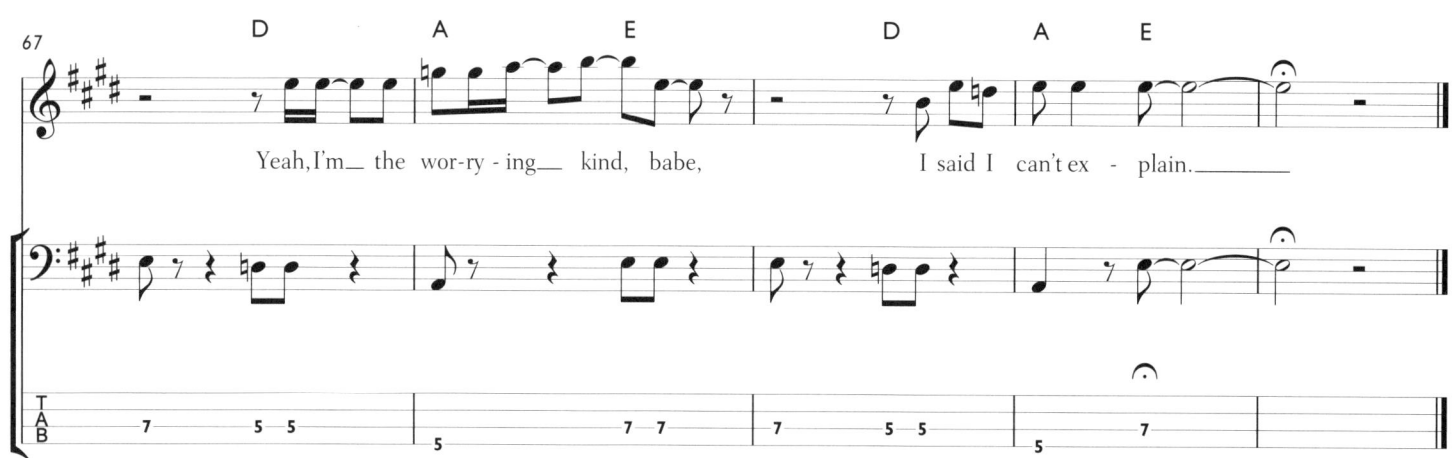

THE KIDS ARE ALRIGHT

Words and Music by Pete Townshend

© 1966 Fabulous Music Ltd

MY GENERATION

Words and Music by Pete Townshend

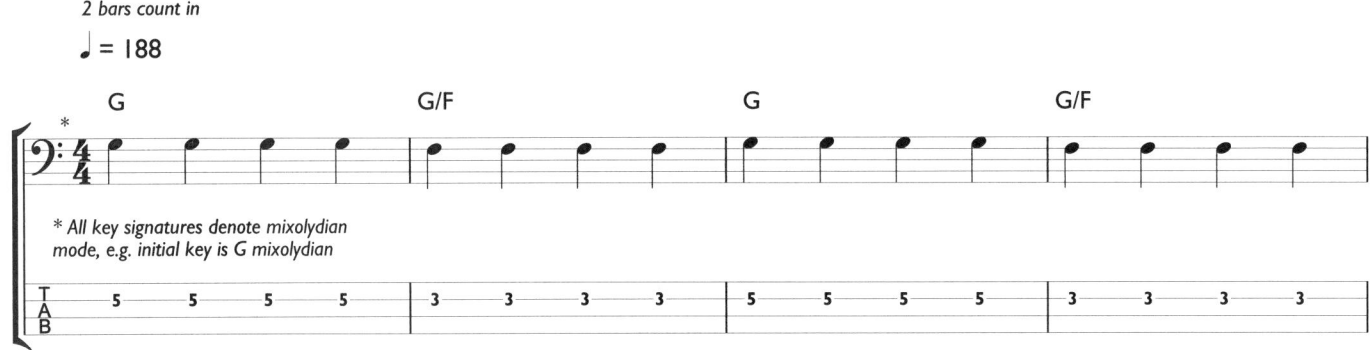

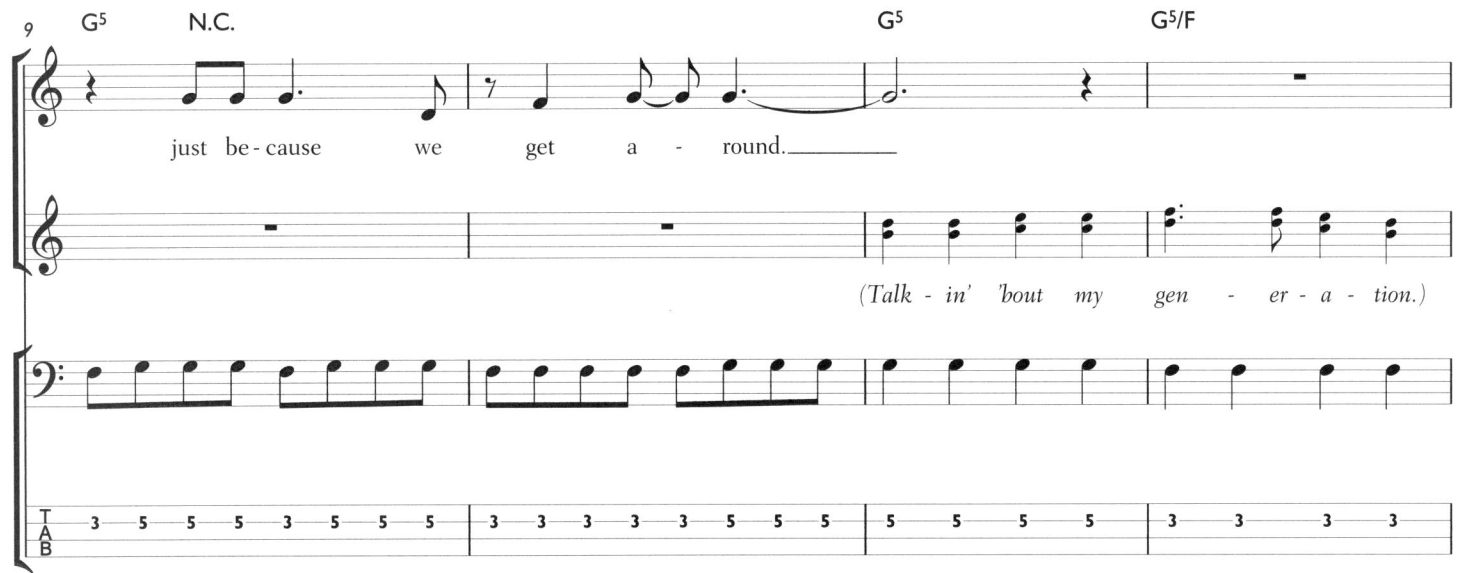

© 1965 Fabulous Music Ltd

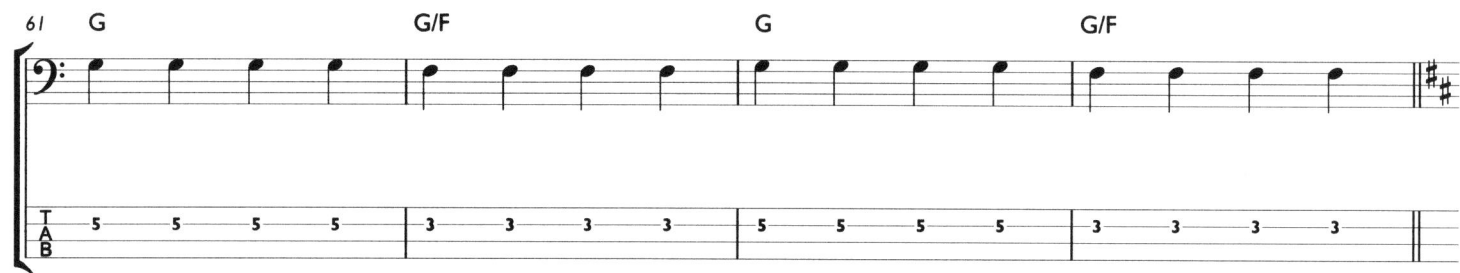

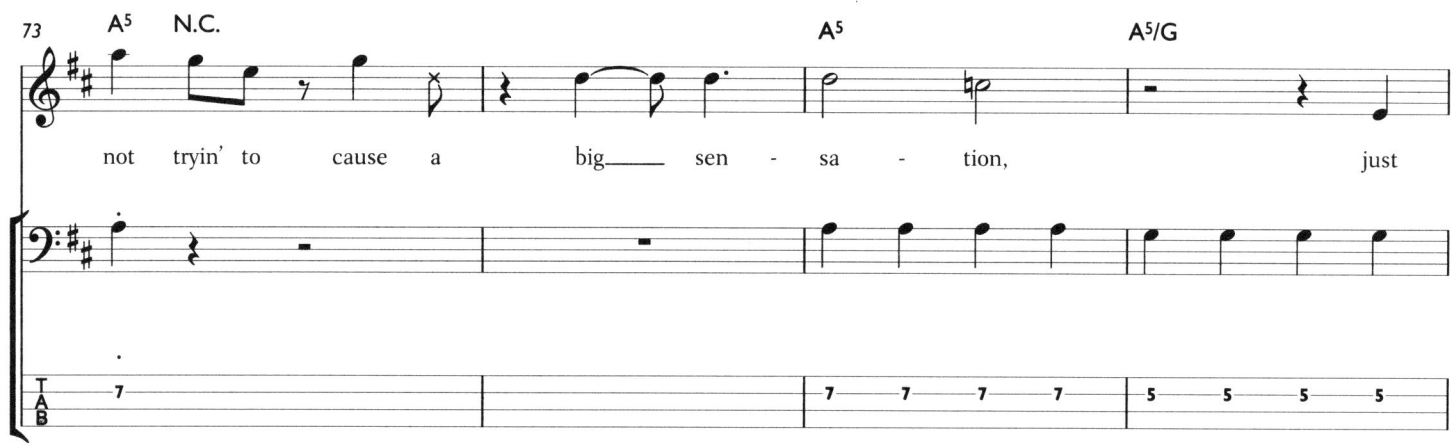

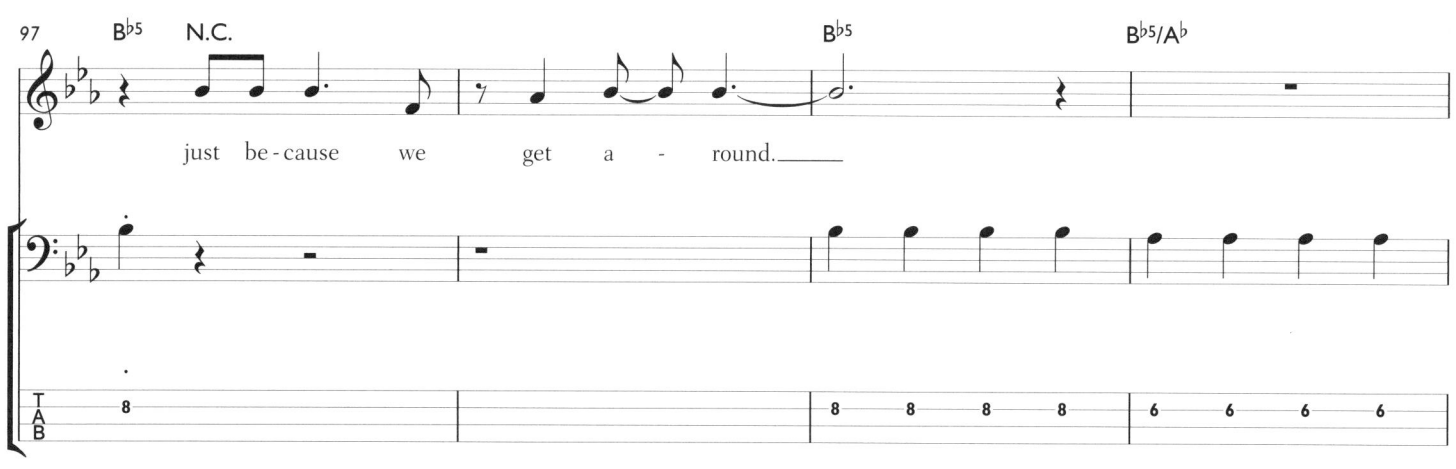
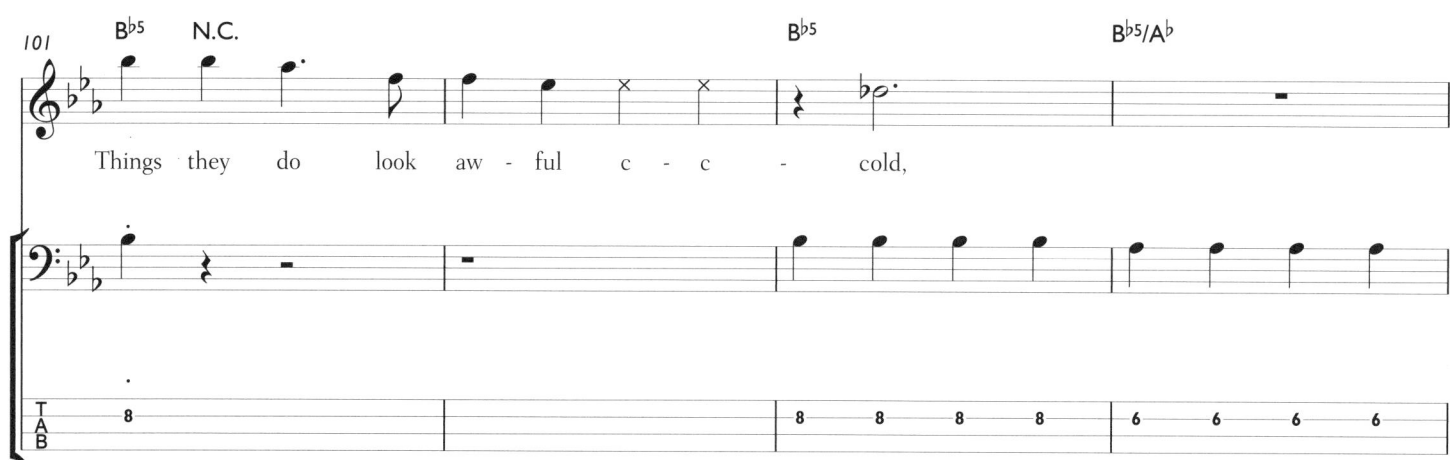

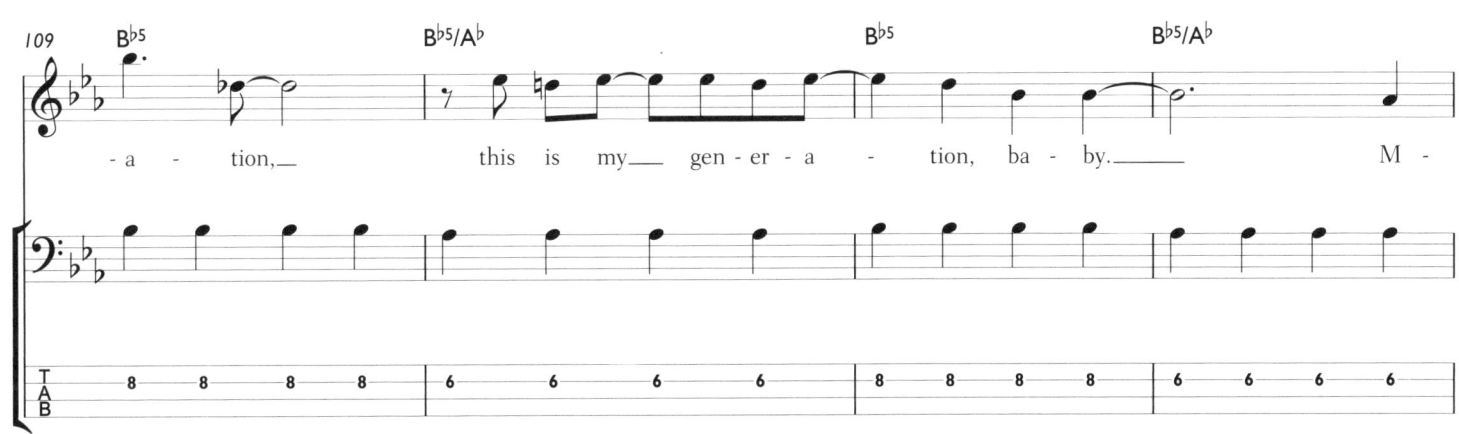
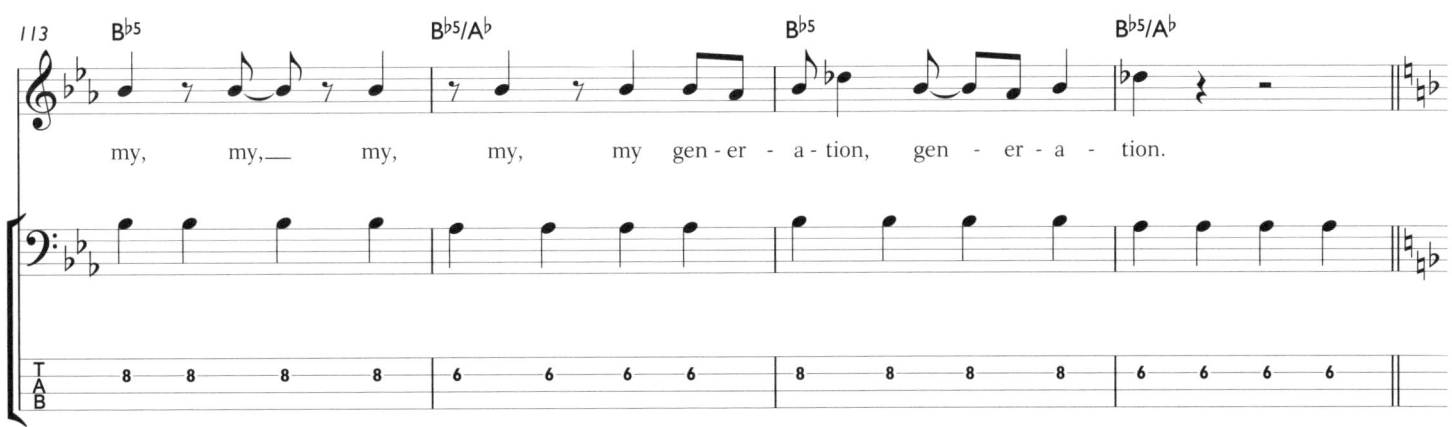
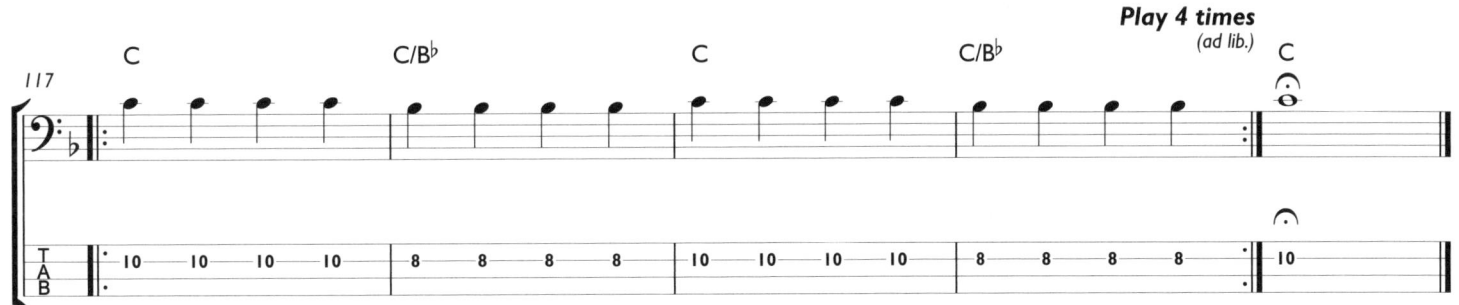

TRACK 10
BACKING TRACK 11

PINBALL WIZARD

Words and Music by Pete Townshend

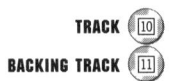

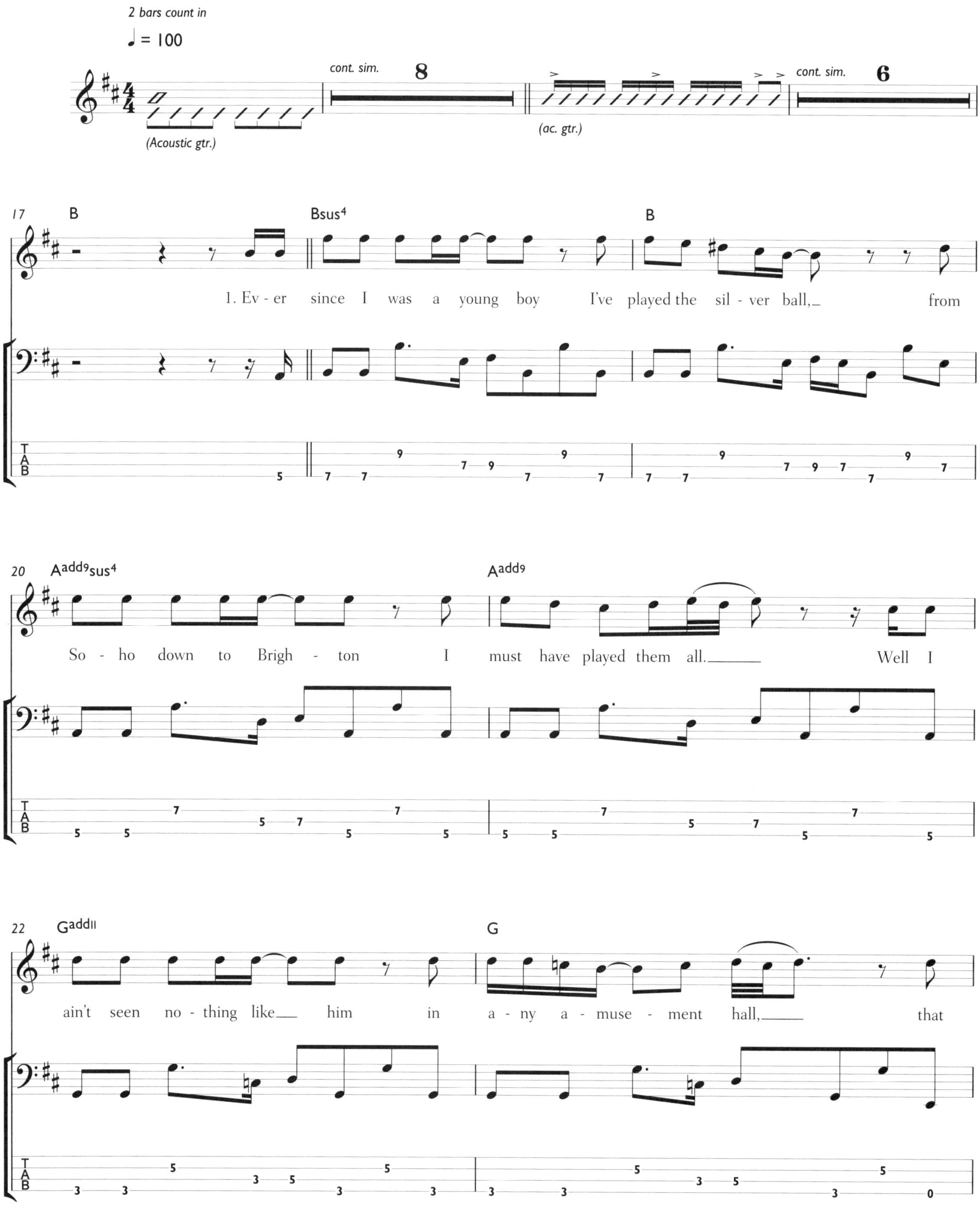

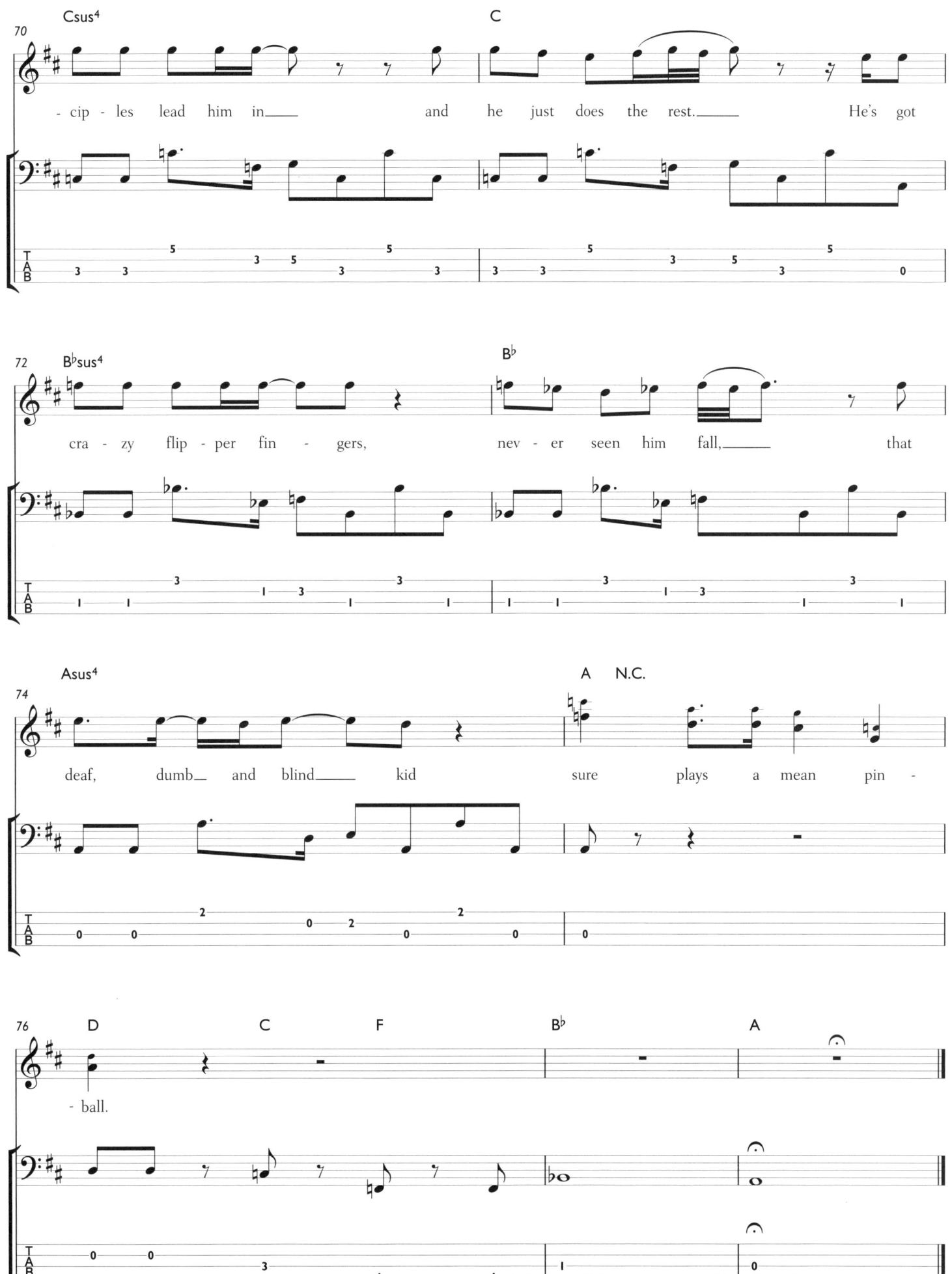

SUBSTITUTE

Words and Music by Pete Townshend

© 1966 Fabulous Music Ltd

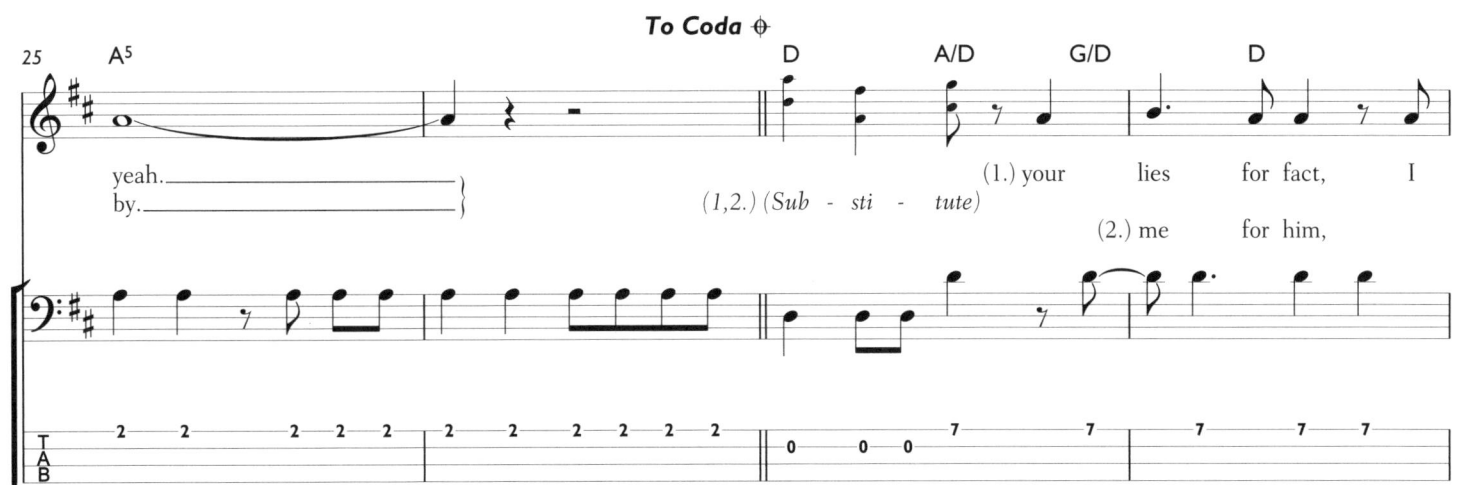

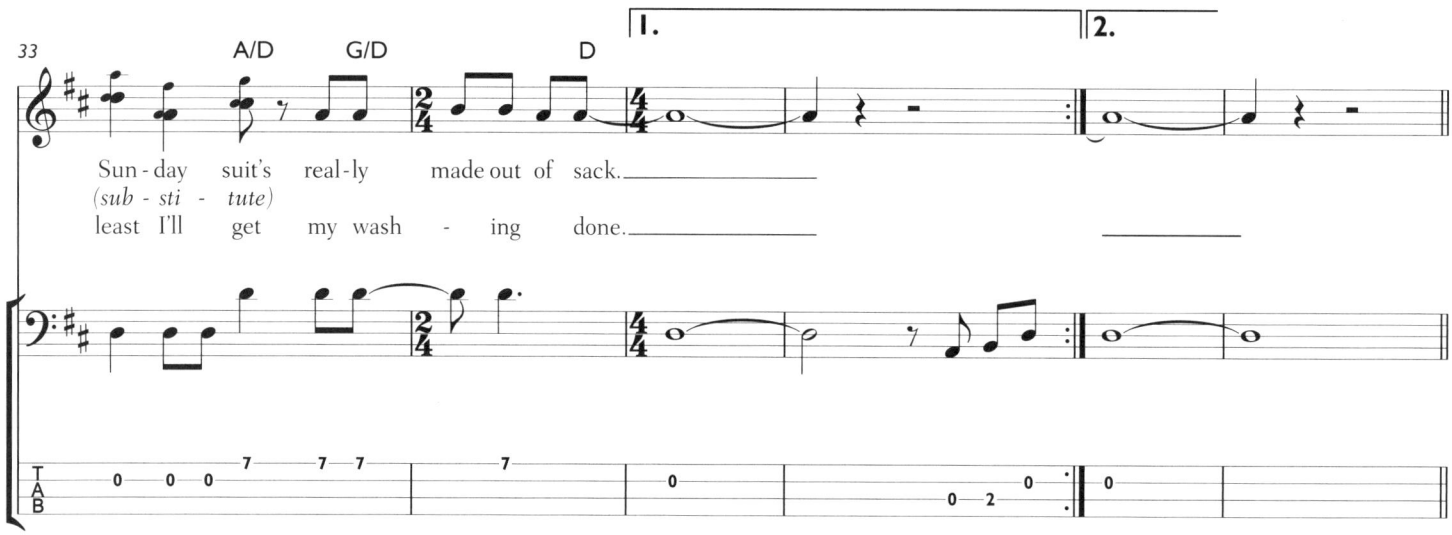
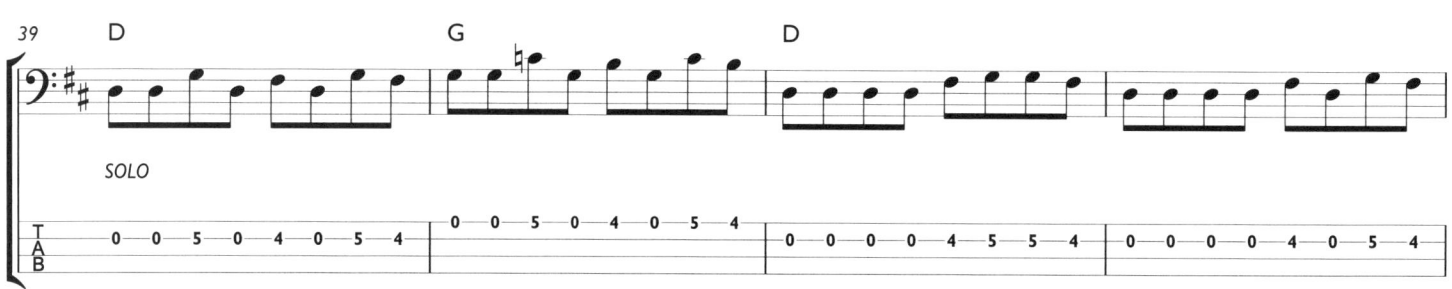
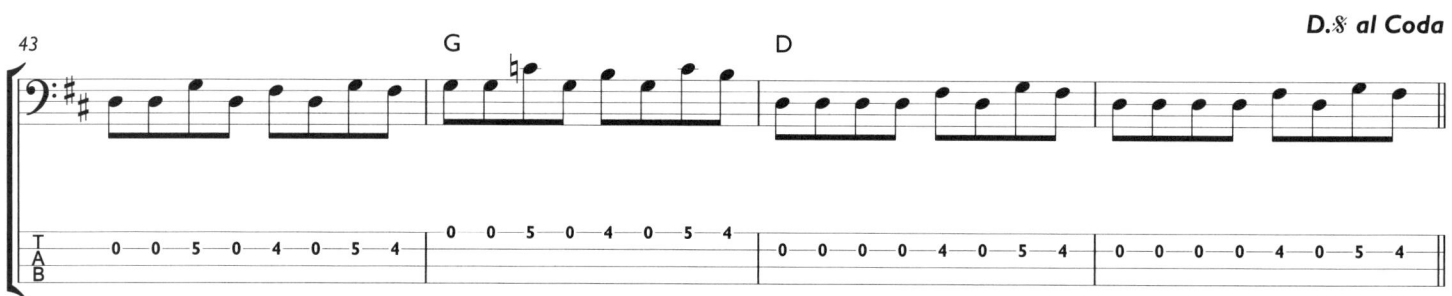

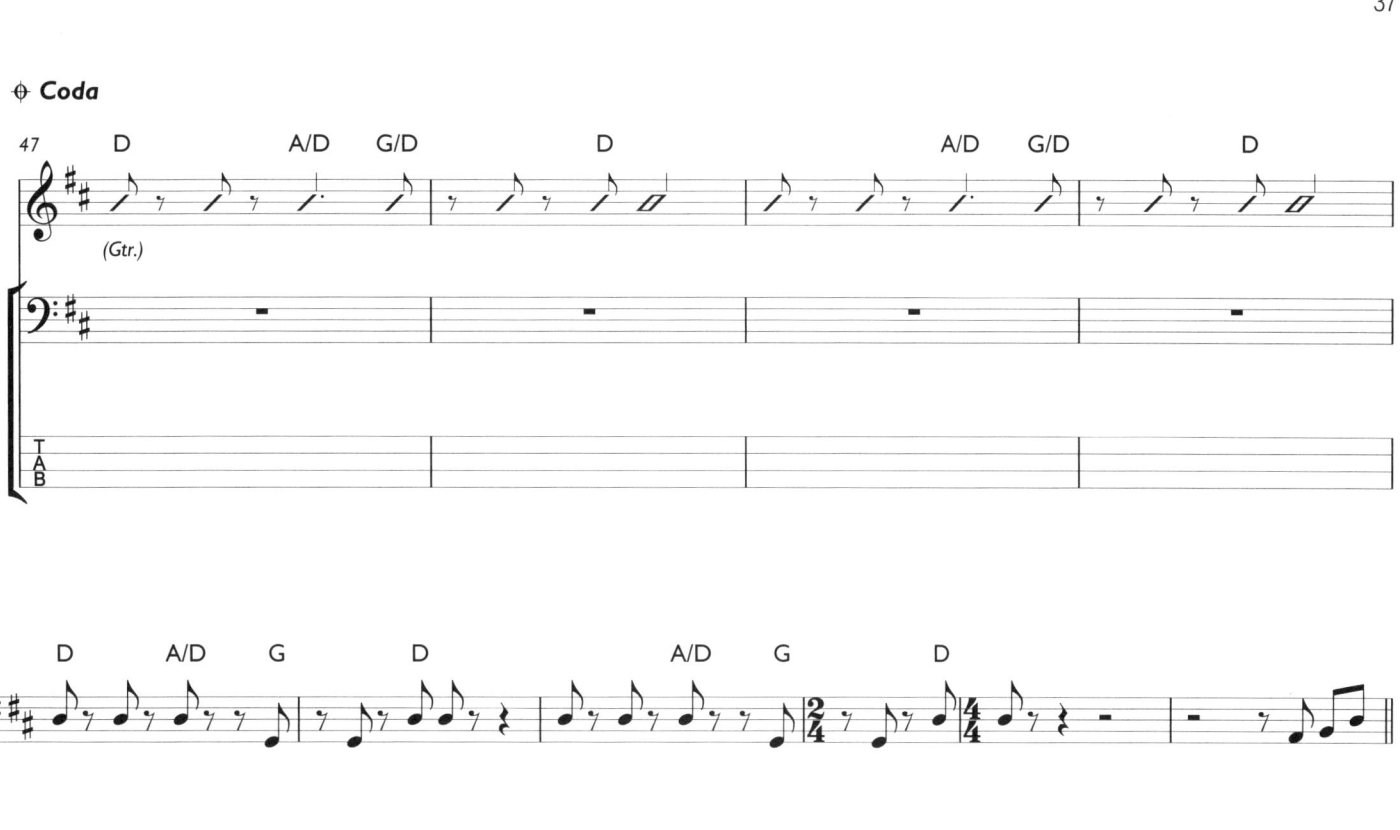
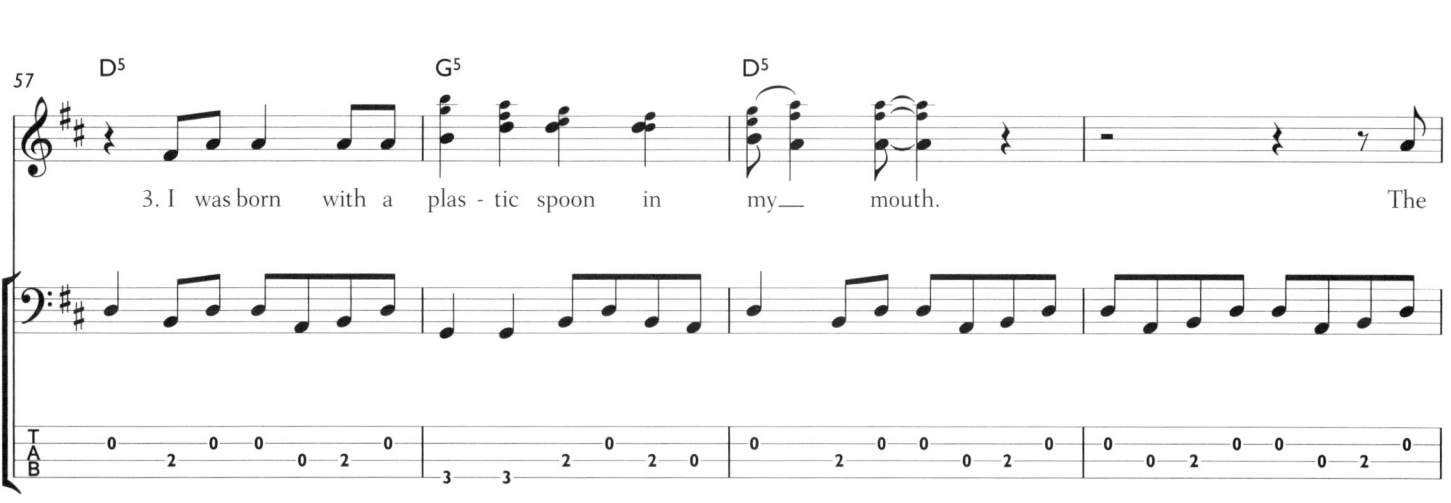
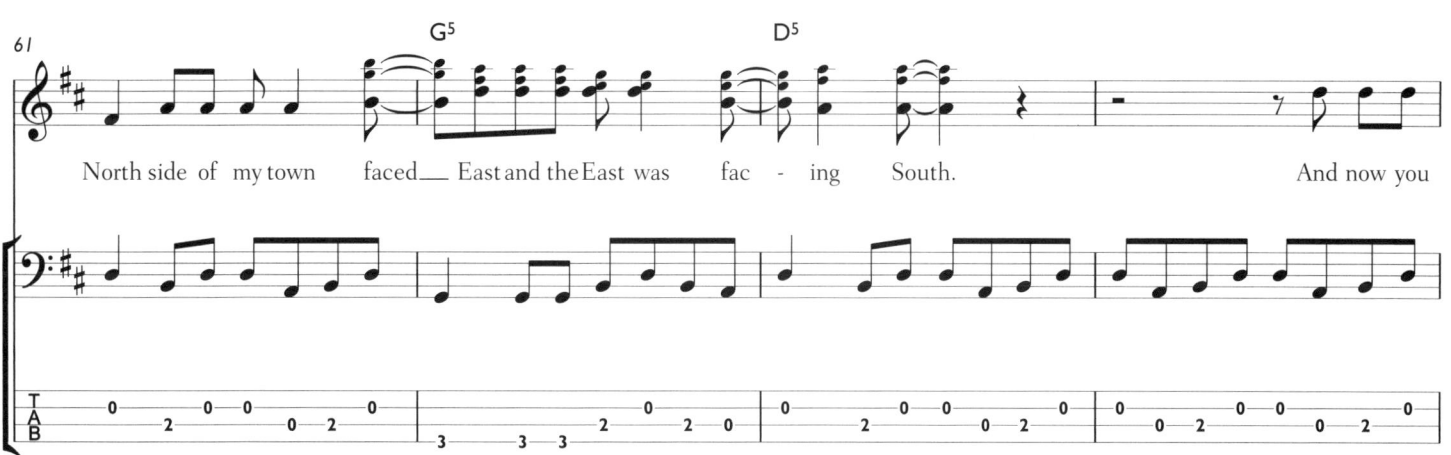

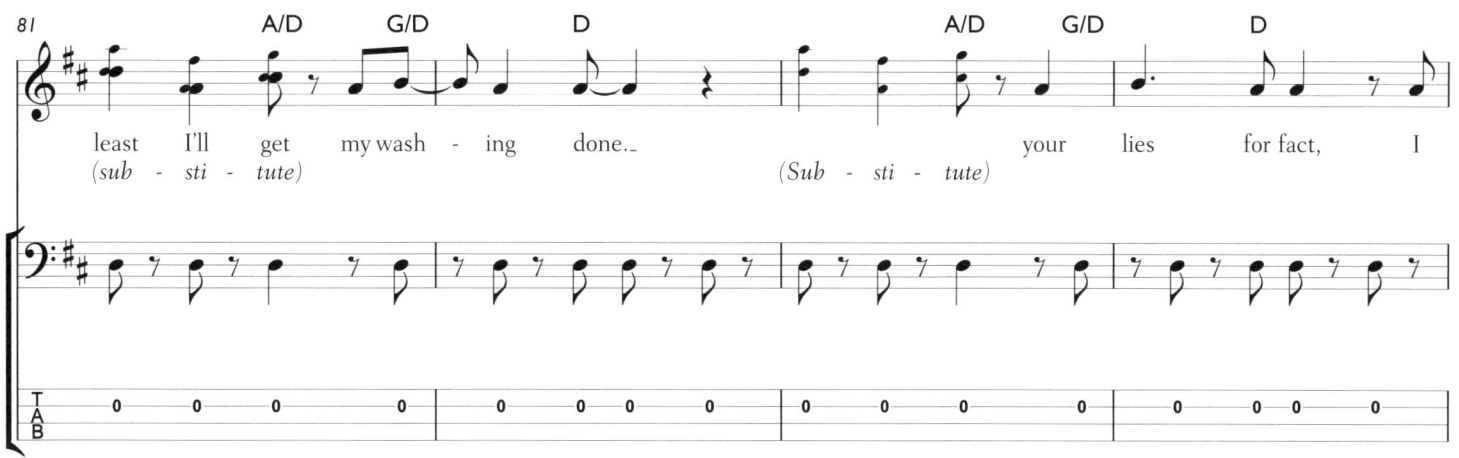

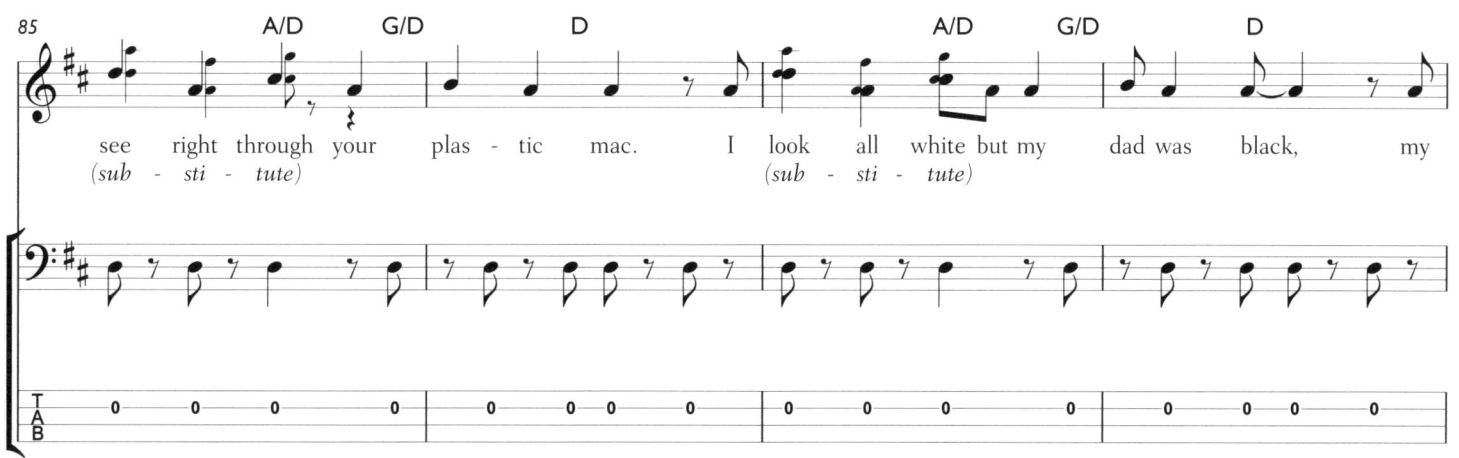

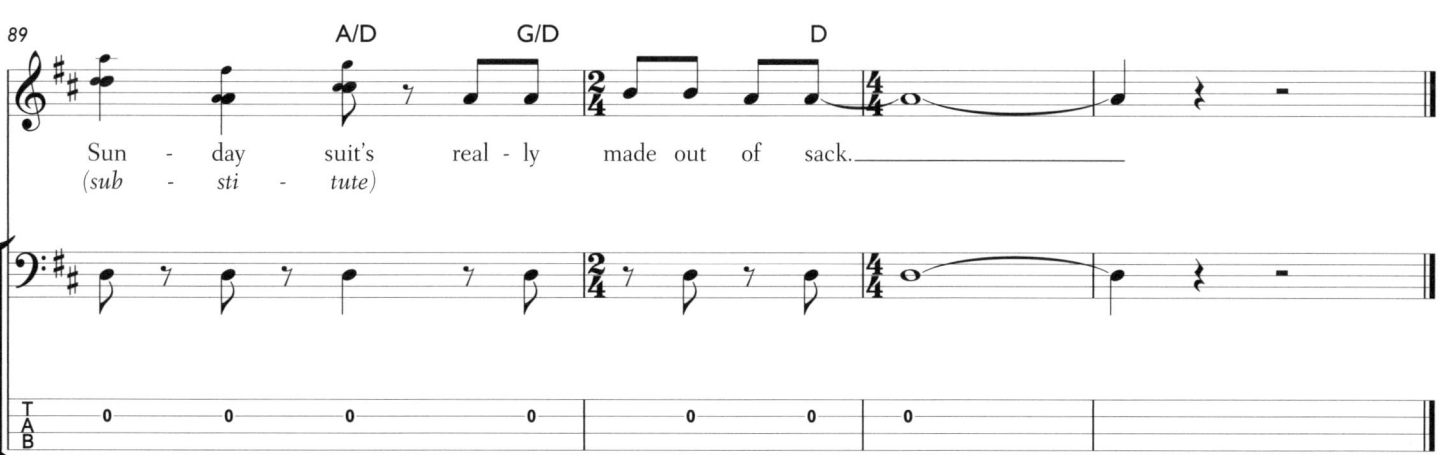

PICTURES OF LILY

Words and Music by Pete Townshend

© 1967 Fabulous Music Ltd

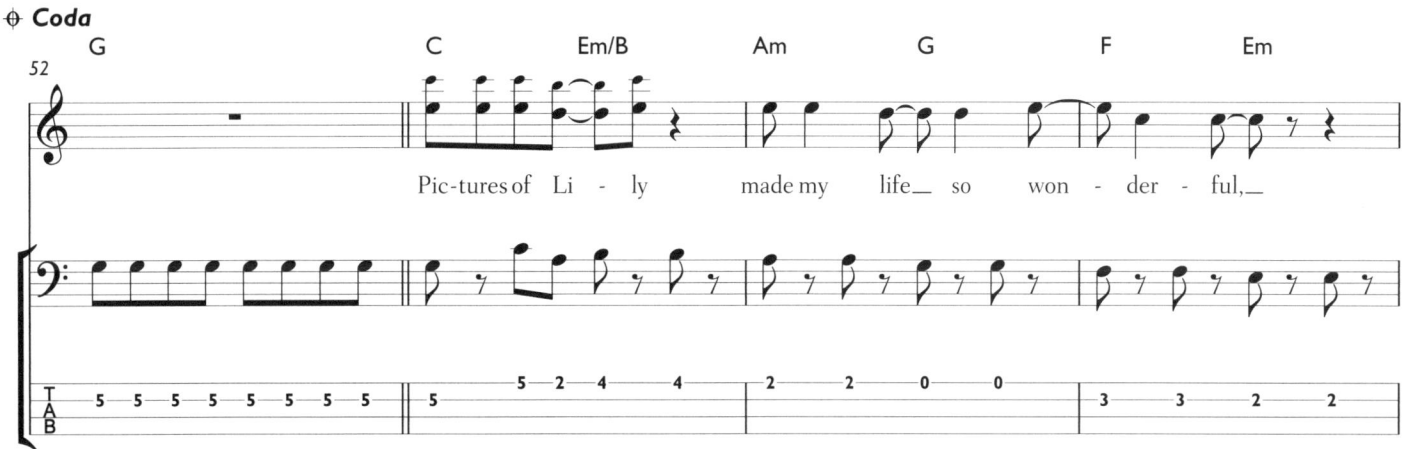
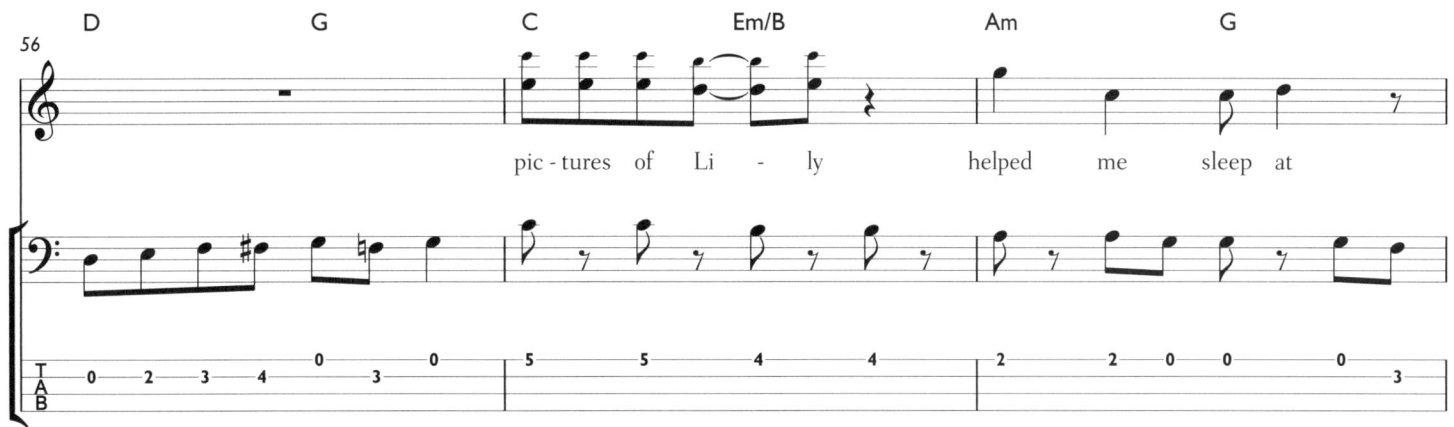

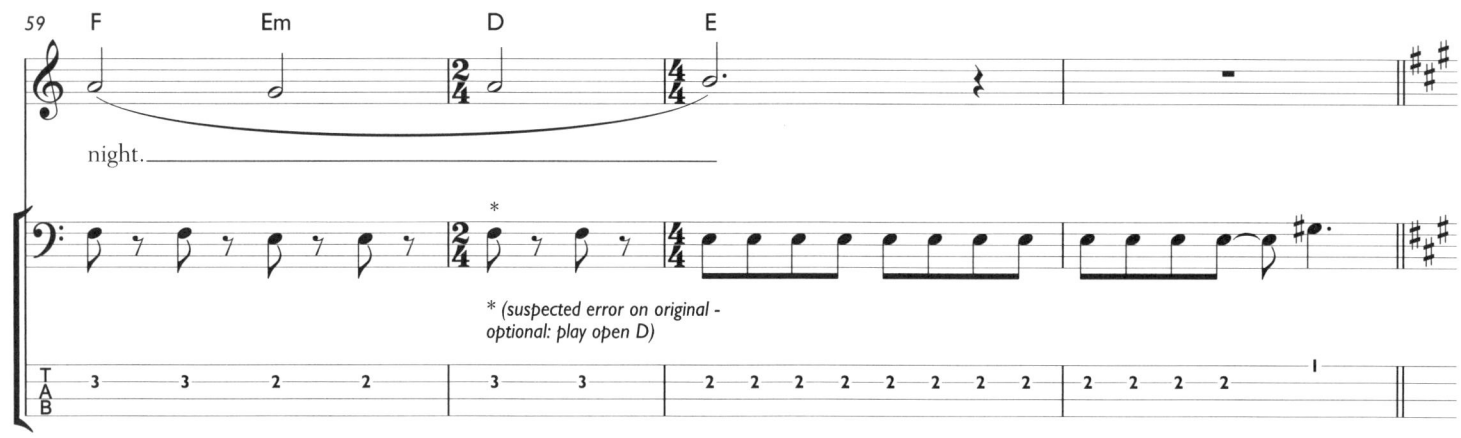

WON'T GET FOOLED AGAIN

Words and Music by Pete Townshend

© 1971 Fabulous Music Ltd

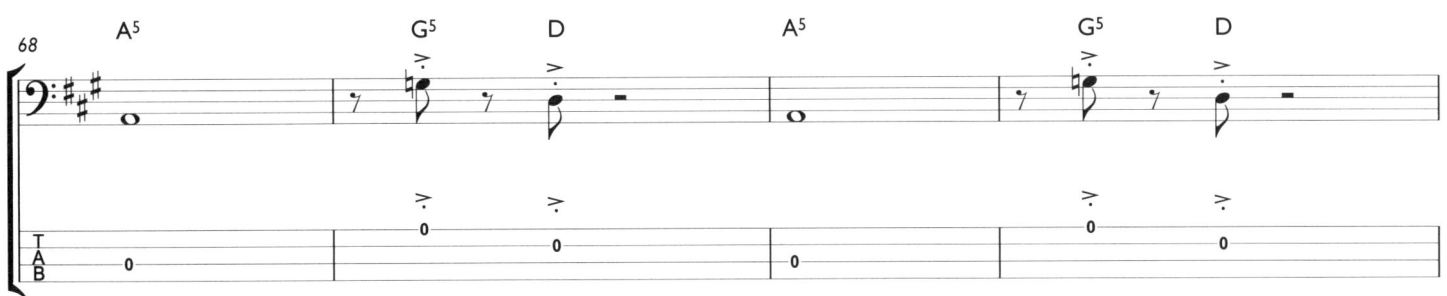
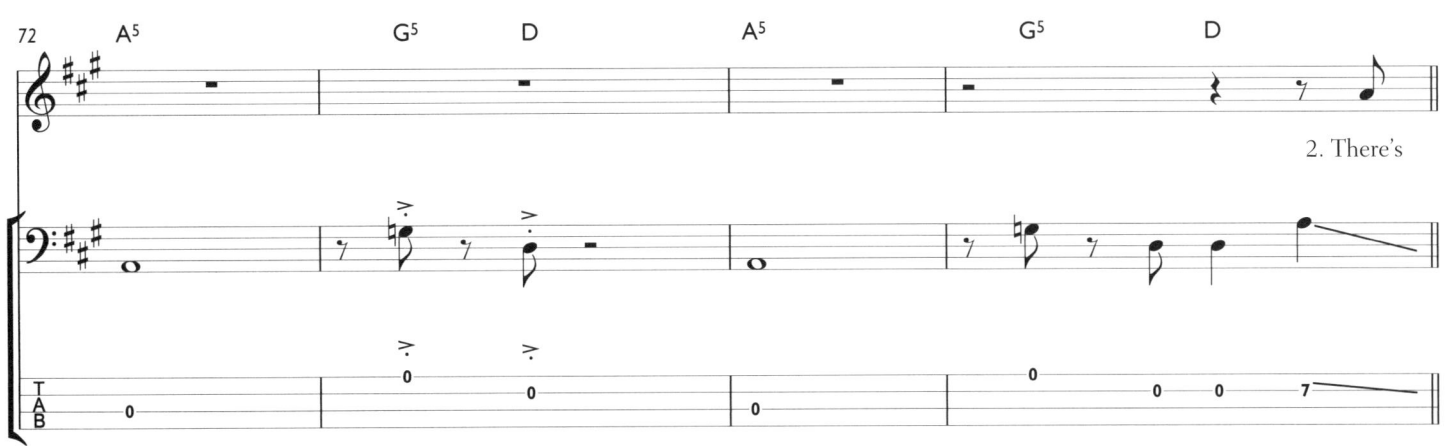
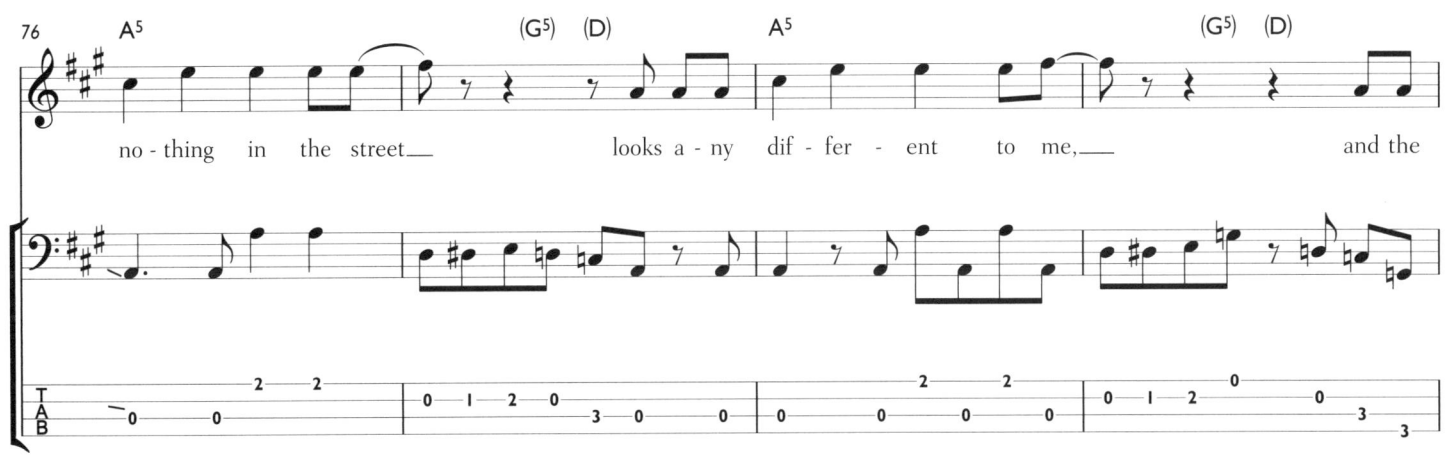
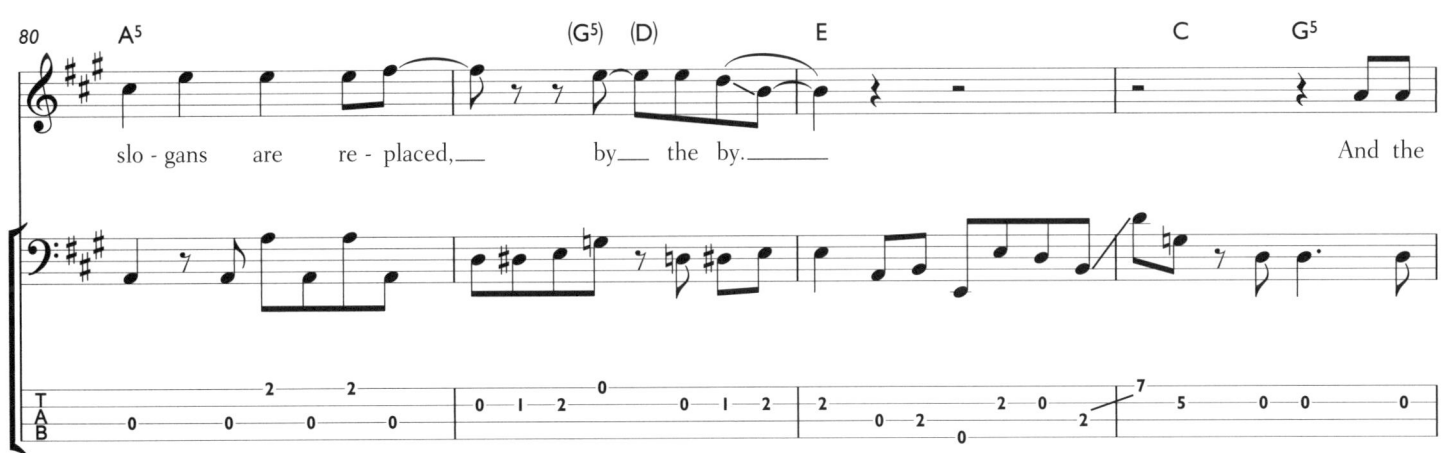

Notation and Tablature explained

Tuning your Bass
The best way to tune your bass is to use an electronic tuner.
Alternatively, you can use relative tuning—this will ensure that your bass is in tune with itself, but won't guarantee that you will be in tune with the original track (or any other musicians).

How to use relative tuning
Fret the low E string at the 5th fret and pluck—compare this with the sound of the open A string. The two notes should be in tune- if not, adjust the tuning of the A string until the two notes match.
Repeat this process for the other strings.

Detuning
If the song uses an unconventional tuning, it will say so clearly at the top of the music, e.g. 'detune bass down by a semitone' or '4 = D' (tune string 4 to D). The standard notation will always be in the key at which the song sounds, but the bass tab will take tuning changes into account. Just detune and follow the fret numbers.
The chord symbols will show the sounding chord above and the chord in which you are actually playing below in brackets.

Use of figures
In order to make the layout of scores clearer, figures that occur several times in a song will be numbered, e.g. 'Fig. 1', 'Fig. 2', etc.
A dotted line underneath shows the extent of the 'figure'. When the phrase is to be played, it will be marked clearly in the score, along with the instrument that should play it.

Reading Bass Tab
Bass tablature illustrates the four strings of the bass, graphically showing you where you put your fingers for each note or chord. It is always shown with a stave in standard musical notation above it. The bass tablature stave has four lines, each of them representing a different string. The top line is the high G string, the second line being the D string, and so on. Instead of using note heads, bass tab uses numbers which show the fret number to be stopped by the left hand. The rhythm is indicated underneath the tab stave. The example (below) shows four examples of single notes and two bass chords.

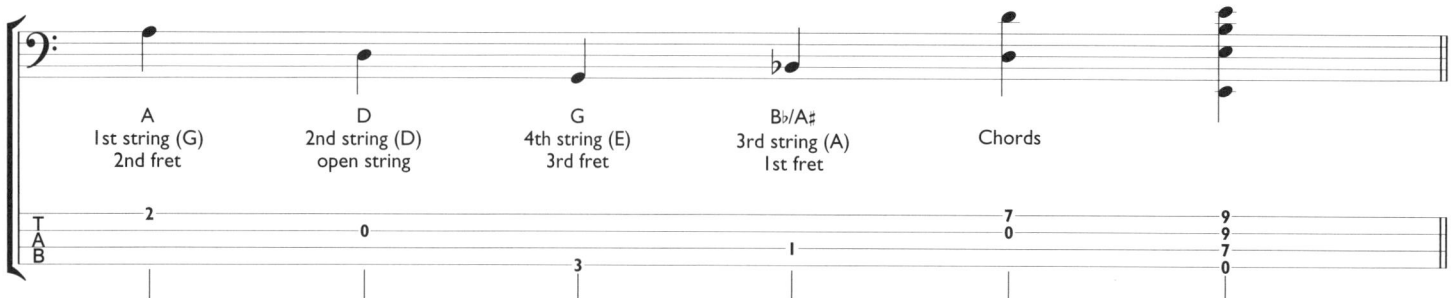

Notation of other bass techniques

Picking hand techniques:

1. Down and up strokes
These symbols show that the first and third notes are to be played with a down stroke of the pick and the others up strokes.

2. Palm mute
Mute the notes with the palm of the picking hand by lightly touching the strings near the bridge.

3. Pick rake
Drag the pick across the indicated strings with a single sweep. The extra pressure will often mute the notes slightly and accentuate the final note.

4. Arpeggiated chords
Strum across the indicated strings in the direction of the arrow head of the wavy line.

5. Tremolo picking
Shown by the slashes on the stem of the note. Very fast alternate picking. Rapidly and continuously move the pick up and down on each note.

6. Pick scrape
Drag the edge of the pick up or down the lower strings to create a scraping sound.

7. Slap techniques—tapping and popping
A 'T' means you tap or strike the string with your right-hand thumb. A 'P' means you 'pop' the string with your index or middle finger- pluck the string so hard that it falls back against the finger board with a slapping sound.

8. Right hand tapping
'Tap' onto the note indicated by a '+' with a finger of the picking hand. It is nearly always followed by a pull-off to sound the note fretted below.

9. Tap slide
As with tapping, but the tapped note is slid randomly up the fretboard, then pulled off to the following note.

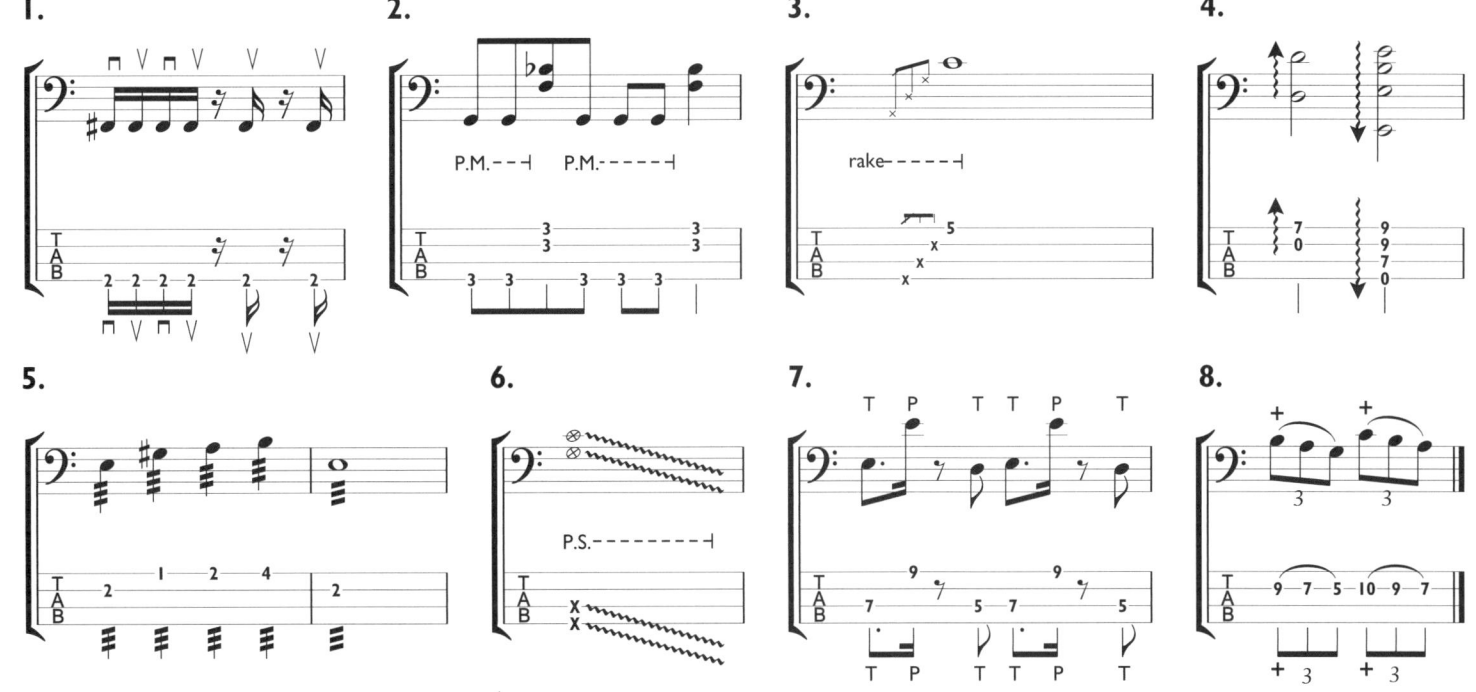

Fretting hand techniques:

1. Hammer-on and pull-off
These consist of two or more notes linked together by a slur. For hammer-ons, fret and play the lowest note, then 'hammer on' to the higher note with another finger. For a pull-off, play the highest note then 'pull off' to a lower note fretted with another finger. In both cases, only pick the first note.

2. Glissandi (slides)
Fret and pick the first note, then slide the finger up to the second note. If they are slurred together, do not re-pick the second note.

3. Slow glissando
Play the note(s) and slowly slide the finger(s) in the direction of the diagonal line(s).

4. Quick glissando
Play the note(s) and immediately slide the finger(s) in the direction of the diagonal line(s).

5. Trills
Play the note and rapidly alternate between this note and the nearest one above in the key signature. If a note in brackets is shown before, begin with this note.

6. Fret hand muting
Mute the notes with cross noteheads with the fretting hand.

7. Left hand tapping
Sound the note by tapping or hammering on to the note indicated by a 'o' with a finger of the fretting hand.

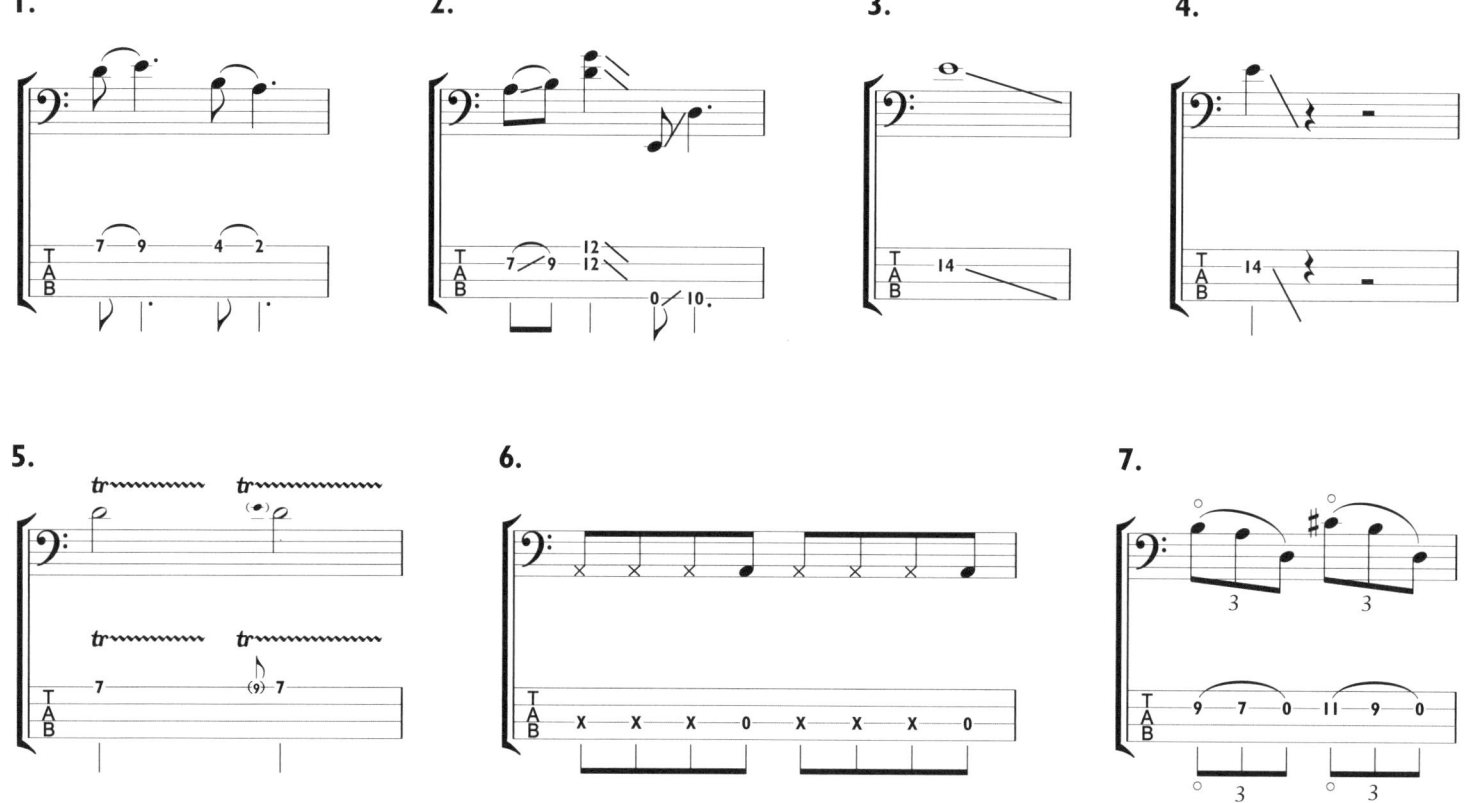

THE AUTHENTIC PLAYALONG SERIES FROM FABER MUSIC

Deep Purple Authentic Bass Playalong/CD	0-571-53132-6	R.E.M. Authentic Bass Playalong/CD	0-571-52930-5
Green Day Authentic Bass Playalong/CD	0-571-52546-6	The Who Authentic Bass Playalong/CD	0-571-53164-4
Guns n' Roses Authentic Bass Playalong/CD	0-571-52750-7	*various artists:*	
Nirvana Authentic Bass Playalong/CD	0-571-52838-4	Classic Rock Authentic Bass Playalong/CD	0-571-52991-7
Pink Floyd Authentic Bass Playalong/2CD	0-571-52667-5	New Rock Anthems Bass Playalong/CD	0-571-52524-5

Faber *ff* Music

To buy Faber Music publications or to find out about the full range of titles available please contact your local music retailer or Faber Music sales enquiries:

Faber Music Ltd, Burnt Mill, Elizabeth Way, Harlow CM20 2HX
Tel: +44 (0) 1279 82 89 82   Fax: +44 (0) 1279 82 89 83
sales@fabermusic.com   fabermusic.com   expressprintmusic.com

ISBN10: 0-571-52943-7
EAN13: 978-0-571-52943-8

To buy Faber Music publications or to find out about the full range of titles available
please contact your local music retailer or Faber Music sales enquiries:

Faber Music Ltd, Burnt Mill, Elizabeth Way, Harlow CM20 2HX
Tel: +44 (0) 1279 82 89 82   Fax: +44 (0) 1279 82 89 83
sales@fabermusic.com   fabermusic.com   expressprintmusic.com